Arctic Lands

CONTENTS

© Aladdin Books Ltd

Designed and produced by
Aladdin Books Ltd
70 Old Compton Street
London W1

Printed in Belgium

First published in
Great Britain in 1986 by
Hamish Hamilton Children's Books
27 Wrights Lane
London W8 5TZ

British Library Cataloguing in Publication Data
Hughes, Jill
    Arctic lands.–(Find out about)
    1. Polar regions – Juvenile literature
    I. Title
    II. Series
    998   G590

    ISBN 0 241 11933 2

Certain illustrations have previously appeared in the "Closer Look"
series published by Hamish Hamilton.

The consultant on this book, JL Cloudsley-Thompson,
is Professor of Zoology, Birkbeck College,
University of London.

FIND OUT ABOUT

Arctic Lands

JILL HUGHES

Illustrated by

R. COOMBS, D. CORDERY
AND M. WILSON

Consultant

J. L. CLOUDSLEY-THOMPSON

Hamish Hamilton · London

The last wild place

The cold lands of the Arctic, stretching around the North Pole from Russia to Greenland, form one of the last wildernesses on Earth. Here there are still huge areas undisturbed by man. At first sight the Arctic looks like a cold desert. For three-quarters of the year snow and ice cover the treeless wastes and icy winds blow over the empty landscape.

However, a closer look reveals that surprising numbers of plants and animals manage to survive and flourish. Some animals and birds spend only part of their time in the Arctic, but others live all the year round in the land of ice and snow.

Musk oxen, Arctic hares and ptarmigans live together in the freezing temperatures of an Arctic winter.

4

Adapting to the Arctic

The plants, insects, birds and animals of the Arctic have all developed ways of combatting the cold. The most obvious defence is a thick, warm coat. The sturdy musk oxen have a double coat of hair — a silky under-layer helps trap air to provide warmth. Other animals have white coats to camouflage them in snow.

The Arctic lands

The Arctic Circle lies around the North Pole at the top of the world. It passes through Canada, Alaska, the Soviet Union, northern Scandinavia and Greenland.

The North Pole itself is covered with a thick, permanent layer of ice and snow. But between this cold, dead region and the "tree-line" — where the northern forests begin — there is a huge belt of land called the tundra. The tundra is covered by snow for three-quarters of the year. No trees grow there, but a large population of plants, animals and birds manages to flourish.

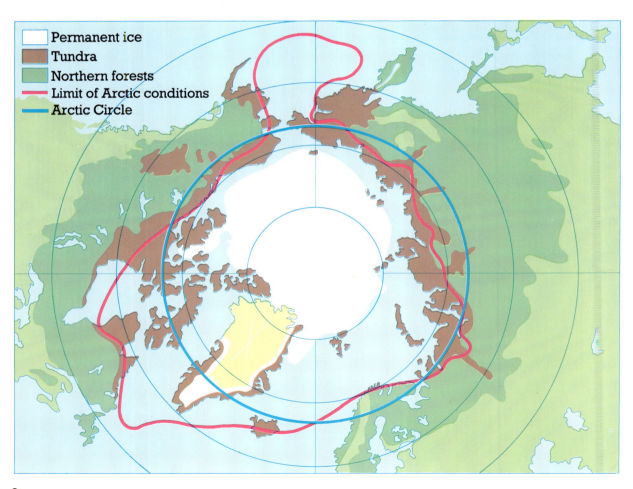

Permanent ice
Tundra
Northern forests
Limit of Arctic conditions
Arctic Circle

Climate

At the North and South Poles the sun hits the Earth at an angle, not directly as it does at the Equator, so it gives less heat. As the Earth spins, it tilts the North Pole away from the sun for half the year: this is the Arctic winter, when the days are short. In the Arctic summer, the Pole is tilted towards the sun and the days are long. But the sun is only strong enough to melt the snow and warm the surface of the Earth. Below a metre or so, the earth is still frozen solid. The frozen area is called the permafrost.

Land, sea and forest

Where the northern edge of the tundra meets the Arctic Ocean, the sea is covered with ice many metres thick for most of the year. The tundra itself is kept moist by water held in the surface layer by the permafrost beneath. In summer, the thaw produces thousands of shallow pools and lakes. Where the permafrost gives way to warmer earth, the forests begin.

Forest

The tree-line is on the southern border of the tundra. There is too little water on the tundra itself for trees to grow because most of it is continuously frozen.

Tundra

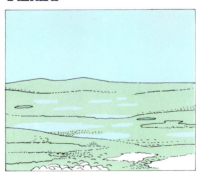

The tundra is not as flat and bare as it may appear. Near the tree-line it is scattered with scrubby vegetation. There are also glens or rocky outcrops and, in summer, streams and lakes.

Coastline

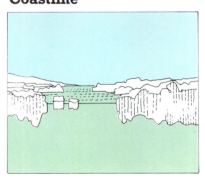

The northern coasts of the Arctic are made up of huge cliffs and flat ice-covered land which stretches for thousands of kilometres. When the sea ice breaks up it makes icebergs.

7

How the land was made

The great ice caps of the North and South Poles were formed about three million years ago during one of the world's ice ages. At this time the northern continents of Eurasia (or Europe and Asia), North America and Greenland moved in a tight ring round the North Pole. The sea there froze over.

The closeness of the continents to the North Pole affected the kind of animals that live in the Arctic today by providing warm "corridors" along which they could travel. This is why there are animals like wolves and bears in the Arctic but not in the Antarctic.

This section across an Arctic landscape shows, from the top, the ice cap, (1) then tundra (2) with pingos (3) and eskers (4), and finally forest (5).

Pingos are like small volcanoes but they were forced up by ice and contain blue ice not lava.

Eskers are the remains of streams which once flowed under ice-sheets. When the ice retreated the stream courses were left higher than the land around.

Pingo

Eskers

The surface of the land

As the ice thaw began, the ice retreated north and concentrated round the Pole. Lichen grew on the gravel left behind by the ice. Soon mosses and other plants followed and a thin soil was laid down. As more plants and animals colonised the Arctic, their bodies enriched the tundra when they died.

Many strange geological lumps and bumps survive on the tundra surface today. They are reminders of how it was formed by the movement of ice and the continual freezing and thawing of the ground.

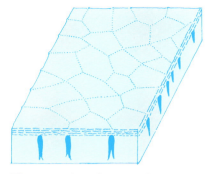

The continual partial thawing and freezing of land cause it to crack into a pattern of multi-sided shapes like "crazy paving".

The edge of a moving glacier, a river of ice, pushes earth and stone in front of it.

Eventually glaciers carve out whole valleys as they sweep through the mountains of ice.

4

5

The closer the ice gets to the tree-line, the warmer the ground is. Here there are pools of melted ice.

The Arctic summer sees the birth of millions of flying and crawling insects that feed on the plant and animal life of the tundra.

The Bumblebee is the only bee able to survive in the Arctic.

Mosquitoes breed in the tundra pools created by the summer thaw.

Blackfly breed in water and provide food for birds in summer.

Many Arctic butterflies have hairs which keep them dry.

Dwarf forms of southern plants like buttercups, lupins and poppies grow on the tundra. Berries provide food for birds and animals.

Mountain aven

Sedge

Arctic rhododendron

Arctic poppy

Arctic willow

Cloudberry

Cranberry

Crowberry

Bilberry

Tundra plants

There are no tall Arctic plants. The growing season is too short to allow trees to grow and there is too little water. Arctic plants grow close to the ground for protection against the icy winds and to suck up every drop of moisture in summer.

Strategies for survival

Arctic plants flower during the brief summer, which lasts from about mid-June to mid-August. Then the tundra blooms with bright pink saxifrage and carpets of yellow Arctic poppy. The tightly packed, low-growing layers of plant life help to trap warm air in the few centimetres above the ground. They create a "micro-climate" of their own where buds can grow in warmth. The micro-climate also supports whole populations of insects which help to pollinate the flowers. Some plants flower and die the same summer; others take years to complete their growth.

Saxifrage

Saxifrages are brilliantly coloured flowers which grow by sending out long shoots. These produce buds in autumn that can live through the winter.

Lichens and mosses are low-growing, tough little plants that can survive beneath snow. Mosses cling to the thin soil with long root systems, using their leaves to absorb water.

Moss

Reindeer moss

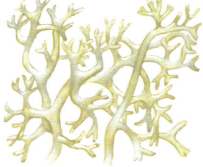

Reindeer moss is a kind of lichen which is eaten by reindeer in Lapland and caribou in North America.

Lichen

Arctic animals

Most of the birds and animals of the Arctic are larger than their relatives from warmer climates. The larger a body is, the more heat it produces. The more compact it is, the more slowly that heat is lost. So Arctic animals also have smaller ears and muzzles and shorter legs which reduce heat loss.

Keeping out the cold

Arctic animals and birds have thick coats of fur or feathers. The coats of caribou are good at keeping them warm. The individual hairs are hollow, to trap air for warmth.

Like musk oxen, caribou build up reserves of fat for the long winter. The white coats of many animals radiate less heat than coloured ones and so help to keep them warm.

Wolves, foxes and caribou are out and about all through the winter and have very thick fur coats. Lemmings remain beneath the snow during winter and have thinner, silkier coats.

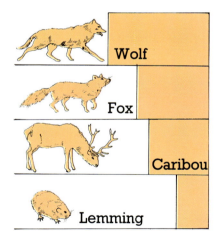

Wolf

Fox

Caribou

Lemming

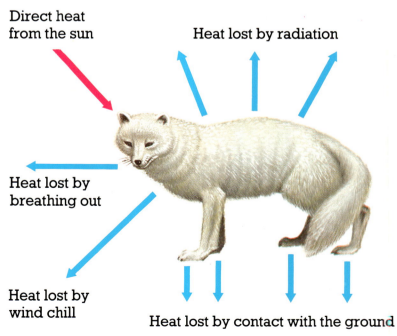

Direct heat from the sun

Heat lost by radiation

Heat lost by breathing out

Heat lost by wind chill

Heat lost by contact with the ground

The picture, right, shows the main ways in which animals lose heat.

The feet of Arctic animals are broad so that they do not sink into snow. Often the soles are covered with fur or feathers.

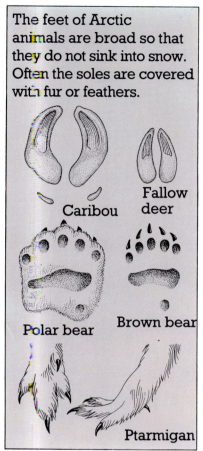

Caribou

Fallow deer

Polar bear

Brown bear

Ptarmigan

The shaggy outer coat of the musk ox covers an undercoat of very warm, short wool.

Arctic animals tend to have shorter ears, noses and tails, and smaller bodies than animals from warmer climates. The long ears of the Desert fox and the Desert hare radiate heat; those of the Arctic animals help to conserve it.

Desert fox

Red fox

Arctic fox

Desert hare

Hare

Arctic hare

Food in the Arctic

Animals and birds that live all year on the tundra are linked by a food chain: the sun makes plants grow; some animals (herbivores) eat the plants and, in the final link, other animals (carnivores) eat the plant-eaters.

Permanent inhabitants

Many animals and birds, like the caribou or the snow geese, leave the tundra in winter for warmer feeding grounds. But a hardy group of creatures lives permanently in the Arctic, like the snowy owl and Arctic fox.

Wolves hunt in packs, foxes usually alone. The Snowy owl and the gyrfalcon will eat lemmings and smaller birds. Ravens are scavengers who will eat anything.

Arctic wolf

Gyrfalcon

Arctic fox

Snowy owl

Raven

Stoat

All these animals live on grasses, leaves, berries and mosses. The tiny vole eats insects too.

Redpoll

Meadow vole

Ptarmigan

Lemming

Arctic hare

Musk ox

Plant-eaters

All the Arctic inhabitants eat as much as they can in summer when food is plentiful. They build up their strength for the long winter. But some plant-eaters manage to find lichen, moss or a few twigs under the snow cover even in winter. The musk oxen, who graze on the lush vegetation of the tundra in summer, paw through the snow crust to get at the lichen which forms their winter diet. Tiny lemmings eat the dormant buds of plants under the snow and Arctic hares burrow for buried vegetation.

Meat-eaters

Meanwhile above ground, wolves, Arctic foxes, owls and ravens roam hungrily in search of prey. All of them will eat carrion, dead animals, if they can. Sometimes they venture to the edge of the sea ice to eat the remains of seals caught by polar bears. They are always on the lookout for weak or injured animals to attack. Stoats and ermines can wriggle down holes after lemmings but they will also attack Arctic hares twice their size.

The hunters

The animal hunters of the Arctic are strong and swift, able to run down or suddenly overpower their prey. They are armed with powerful teeth and claws. But they also have to compete with one another for their food.

Teamwork

Wolves are social animals. They live and hunt together in packs, obeying a leader. They will run down their prey, taking it in turns to keep up the chase until the victim is exhausted.

The Arctic wolves live mainly on caribou, following the herds wherever they go, looking out for calves or sick animals who may fall behind the rest of the herd.

Wolves may attack the powerful musk oxen but these animals then form themselves into a defensive semicircle, facing outwards. With the calves safely in the centre, the wolves slink away.

The Timber or Grey wolf is found all over the Arctic.

If a caribou bull turns and makes a stand, wolves will usually not dare to attack.

Other visitors from the forests come to the tundra in search of food.

The wolverine is a large and particularly ferocious member of the weasel family.

The lynx comes to the tundra in winter, to find hare, lemmings and voles.

The red fox is only seen on the tundra in summer.

The grizzly bear lives in the northern forests but is found on the tundra in summer, when it gorges itself on berries and fish as well as on small animals and carrion.

The caribou herds

Caribou in North America and domesticated reindeer in Europe are the deer of the north. Their beautiful, thick, grey-beige coats give very efficient protection against the cold. Their large hooves are split to give a broad base for walking on soft snow. The hooves also have sharp edges for chipping through ice and snow to get at the lichen which is the main food of the deer.

Caribou live in very large herds, following a leader, a senior bull caribou. They spend the winter in the forests and migrate north to the tundra every spring.

On the move

In the spring the caribou begin to stream out from the tree-line in their thousands, following traditional trails north across the tundra. They travel slowly but steadily, each animal treading in the footsteps of the one in front to save energy. When they reach their summer breeding grounds they will have their calves and then spend the rest of the season feeding until it is time to return to the forests.

The Barren Grounds

The largest herds of caribou are found on the Canadian Barren Grounds, vast, flat treeless plains that stretch from Alaska to Labrador. After a summer on the Barrens, the caribou are well-fed and have shining coats. The bulls, with long white manes and magnificent antlers, fight for the privilege of leading the herds for the next year.

The lemmings

The brown lemming is one of the two most common types of lemming. About 12 cm (5 in) long, it lives mainly in the sedge meadows on the tundra.

Lemmings are small, brown rodents and they breed in large numbers in the Arctic. They live in underground burrows, feeding on buds and shoots and spending much of the winter asleep. They are the favourite food of almost every predator in the Arctic.

Population explosion

It used to be thought that when the lemming population got too big, the lemmings would commit mass suicide by jumping over cliffs. This is now known to be untrue.

However, the size of the population has a dramatic effect on the lives of other animals in the Arctic food chain. Every four years or so the number of lemmings goes up. Some emigrate, while others provide extra food for predators like owls and foxes. These creatures in their turn produce larger numbers of young.

The collared lemming lives in the drier slopes and raised areas of the tundra. Its coat turns white in winter.

Lemmings and owls

During a "peak" year for lemmings, snowy owls build their nests in areas where they find the most lemmings. Research has shown that the owls may not breed at all if there are not enough lemmings.

The male owl catches lemmings and "presents" them to the female as an encouragement for her to nest. When she has laid her eggs and is sitting on the nest, he again brings her a steady supply of lemming "gifts". In a good year the female owl will lay seven to nine eggs. The female has grey and brown flecked plumage; the male is white.

Male snowy owl with chick: the chick's mottled grey down camouflages it well against the grey, lichen-covered stones of its nest site.

Spring arrivals

In May, migrating birds begin to arrive to build their nests and lay their eggs. Early birds are snow buntings, Lapland buntings and turnstones. They peck at the edge of the melting snow for emerging insects or seeds. They are weak after their long journey and need to restore their energy quickly so that they can get on with the important job of rearing their young. They are soon followed by geese, swans and loons. In June the Arctic tern appears after the longest migration of all: a journey of thousands of kilometres from the South Pole.

Trumpeter swans

Barnacle goose

Arctic loon

Winter plumage

Common loon

Knot

Sandhill crane

Lesser scaup

Bear goose

Red-breast goose

King eider duck

The sounds of spring

The waterfowl take advantage of the abundant supply of summer food to raise large broods. They nest together as species — barnacle geese choose the high cliffs close to the sea, eider duck prefer the marshy edges of tundra pools. We often think of the Arctic as a silent place, blanketed with snow. In the summer the tundra resounds to the mingled whoops, honks, quacks and "beagle-like yelps" of the barnacle goose as the many wildfowl call to each other, warning of approaching predators.

Below are some of the spring and summer visitors to the Arctic.

Whooper swan

Blue snow goose

Rock pipit

Snow goose

Bewick's swan

Old squaw duck

Northern phalarope

Red phalarope

Arctic summer

Although the Arctic summer is short it is packed with excitement! All sorts of visitors are still arriving and regular inhabitants, like the caribou and the musk oxen, are out and about, shedding their old winter coats.

The warm sun thaws the cold surface of the tundra, creating thousands of shallow pools. Millions of insects breed in the water and provide a food supply for migrant birds.

The most noticeable change that summer brings is the continuous daylight: in August the days are 24 hours long. Arctic wildlife packs a great deal of activity into this period. Hares and foxes often wait until the softer light of a summer "evening" to come out and hunt, but the birds build their nests, lay their eggs and raise their chicks 24 hours a day.

Visitors and regular inhabitants alike take full advantage of the short Arctic summer.

Sandhill crane

Musk oxen

Arctic fox

Whistling crane

Red-breasted merganser

Ground squirrel

Spectacled eider duck

Squirrels and foxes

As soon as the migrant ducks and geese have laid their eggs, they begin to keep an anxious watch for predators. Ground squirrels and foxes are both on the look-out for birds' eggs and chicks.

The squirrels are true hibernators who spend the winter asleep. They must therefore eat enough now to see them through the winter. They too are prey to the red foxes.

Caribou

Snow geese

Canada geese

Old squaw duck

Chilled by the shorter days,
the Canada geese fly south
for the winter.

Mother grizzly bears
take refuge in dens for
the winter. Here they will
give birth to 2 or 3 cubs
in January or February.

Summer's end

As the days get shorter and the sun begins to drop lower in the sky, summer visitors to the tundra prepare to leave. Most of these are migrating birds. From the end of July these birds begin gathering in large flocks.

The last of the summer weather ripens a crop of berries on the tundra – nourishing food for birds and small mammals, like the ground squirrel, but also for the massive grizzly bear. Animals which will remain on the tundra for winter start to grow their thick winter coats, many of them white to blend in with the snowy landscape.

The ground squirrel sleeps through the months from August to May in a grass-lined underground nest.

After the summer moult, many animals begin to grow their white camouflage coats as autumn comes to an end.

Weasel

Arctic hare

Ptarmigan

Arctic fox

27

The cold time

Life on the tundra in winter is hard and bleak. Even more than the cold, the lack of food is now a threat to the animals and to the few birds, like the redpoll or the ptarmigan, who remain. Arctic hares are still about, bounding over large areas and digging through the snow for any leaves they can find.

While the Arctic foxes cover great distances in search of small mammals or birds to eat, the musk oxen paw the snow to uncover the grass they need to sustain their bulky bodies through this lean time.

The snow on the ground does not turn to liquid. Instead it evaporates to refreeze into the snow above. This way the actual ground stays dry.

28

Under the snow cover

Life underground is warmer than above ground. The temperature here stays just above freezing. Lemmings take advantage of this and live in a network of tunnels not far from the surface. They eat buds and shoots. They are not entirely safe, however, because the slender white ermine can pursue them down their burrows and along the tunnels. Arctic foxes also dig for lemmings and make sudden pounces into the snow to try to scare them out of their holes.

The redpoll survives by storing food in its stomach.

Although the temperature above ground may be as low as −46°C (−51°F) beneath the snow it stays just above freezing point. A layer of air trapped between snow and ground allows tiny creatures like lemmings and voles to live an underground life here through the winter.

Evaporation

People of the Arctic

Thousands of years ago the Inuit, or Eskimos, of Alaska, Canada and Greenland learned to live in the Arctic lands, hunting, fishing and gathering berries and plants. They used the skins of the animals they killed to make warm, waterproof clothes, shelters and boats. In a land where there is little wood, they used bone and stone to make tools.

The Inuit lived a nomadic life – moving from place to place in search of food. They followed the caribou across the tundra in summer and in winter hunted seal.

The Inuit knew their world: their survival depended on following the tracks of animals or judging sudden changes in the weather. Today many of them live in settlements and buy goods from supermarkets.

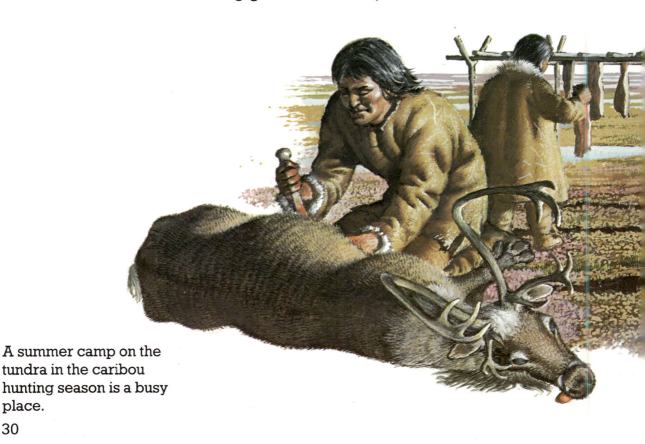

A summer camp on the tundra in the caribou hunting season is a busy place.

A caribou provides more than just meat. Its skin makes warm clothing or a skin tent for summer. The strips of meat are hung to dry so that they will keep longer. The bones will be made into scrapers. Wolverine fur is very waterproof and is used to edge hoods where the moisture from breath condenses in the cold.

Caribou

Ringed seal

Wolverine

Clothes made from skins

Harpoon

Tools for scraping

Glossary

Carnivore   An animal that eats meat.

Evaporation   The process in which water turns into water vapour when it is heated.

Herbivore   An animal that eats plants.

Inuit   The Eskimo people of North America.

Micro-climate   A climate created in a small area, as in the few centimetres between the ground and the tundra vegetation.

Migration   A journey made by an animal, bird or insect to spend a season in another part of the world.

Mammal   Warm-blooded animal, often with a fur coat, which feeds its young with its own milk.

Nomadic life   Moving from place to place in search of food and shelter.

Permafrost   The ground, about a metre below the surface of the tundra, which is permanently frozen.

Tundra   A Lapland word for the stretches of barren land that lie between the permanent polar ice and the northern forests.

Index